THE CAT'S WHISKERS

Also for Pan Macmillan by Katie Wales

SHARK-INFESTED CUSTARD

THE
CAT'S
WHISKERS

by Katie Wales

illustrated by David Farris

PICCOLO

PAN MACMILLAN
CHILDREN'S BOOKS

First published 1993 by Pan Macmillan Children's Books

a division of Pan Macmillan Publishers Limited
Cavaye Place London SW10 9PG
and Basingstoke

Associated companies throughout the world

ISBN 0–330–32877–8

1 3 5 7 9 8 6 4 2

A CIP catalogue record for this book is available from
the British Library

Typeset by Intype, London
Printed by Cox & Wyman Ltd, Reading, Berkshire

Dedi-cat-ed to Chief and Tom-Tom;
and in memory of Snoops and Tomsy

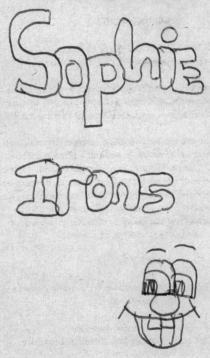

CONTENTS

1

ONCE UPON A TIME:
CATS IN THE WILD

Once upon a time, about thirty-six million years ago, the first cats appeared. One was the sabre-toothed cat, so called because of its two sharp six-inch-long teeth. Ten million years later came our "big cats", as we know them. The domestic cat is probably descended from the African or Kaffir wild cat, which is still found in North Africa. Cats still live in the wild in Scotland. Our cat's other relations are, of course, the lion, tiger, leopard and cheetah (the fastest animal on earth), and also the puma, jaguar, lynx and ocelot. The cat is also related to the mongoose and the aardwolf! There are about fifty kinds of wild cat, all sizes and colours, spotted and striped, from the jungle to the Arctic. They are all meat-eaters (carnivores), and all good hunters and jumpers.

The word "cat" comes from the Latin *cattus*; the wild cat the Romans called *feles*, from which our word "feline" comes. The Romans may have borrowed *cattus* from the Arabic *quittah*, used by passing traders. *Cattus* became *chat* in French, *Katze* in German, *gato* in Spanish, *koshka* in Russian and *kot* in Polish.

Auntie Agnes's Cat

My Auntie Agnes has a cat.
I do not like to tell her that
Its body seems a little large
(With lots of stripes for camouflage).
Its teeth and claws are also larger
Than they ought to be. A rajah
Gave her the kitten, I recall,
When she was stationed in Bengal.
But that was many years ago,
And kittens are inclined to grow.
So now she has a fearsome cat –
But I don't like to tell her that.

Colin West

from *The Cat that Walked by Himself*

by Rudyard Kipling

. . . The Cat said: "I am the Cat who walks by himself and all places are alike to me . . . and I wish to come into your Cave!". . .

Then the Woman laughed and said, "You are the Cat who walks by himself, and all places are alike to you. You are neither a friend nor a servant. You have said it yourself. Go away and walk by yourself in all places alike."

Then Cat pretended to be sorry and said, "Must I never come into the Cave? Must I never sit by the warm fire? Must I never drink the warm white milk? You are very wise and very beautiful. You should not be cruel even to a Cat."

Woman said, "I knew I was wise, but I did not know I was beautiful. So I will make a bargain with you. If I ever say one word in your praise, you may come into the Cave."

"And if you say two words in my praise?" said the Cat.

"I never shall," said the Woman, "but if I say two words in your praise, you may sit by the fire in the Cave."

"And if you say three words?" said the Cat.

"I never shall," said the Woman, "but if I say three words in your praise, you may drink the warm white milk three times a day for always and always and always."

Then the Cat arched his back and said, "Now let the Curtain at the mouth of the Cave, and the Fire at the back of the Cave, and the Milk-pots that stand by the Fire, remember what my Enemy and the Wife of my Enemy has said." And he went away through the Wet Wild Woods waving his wild tail and walking by his wild lone.

That night when the Man and the Horse and the Dog came home from hunting, the Woman did not tell them of the bargain that she had made with the Cat, because she was afraid that they might not like it.

Cat went far and far away and hid himself in the Wet Wild Woods by his wild lone for a long time till the Woman forgot all about him. Only the Bat – the little upside-down Bat – that hung inside the Cave knew where Cat hid; and every evening Bat would fly to Cat with news of what was happening.

One evening Bat said, "There is a Baby in the Cave. He is new and pink and fat and small, and the Woman is very fond of him."

"Ah!" said the Cat, listening. "But what is the Baby fond of?"

"He is fond of things that are soft and tickle," said the Bat. "He is fond of warm things to hold in his arms when he goes to sleep. He is fond of all those things."

"Ah!" said the Cat, listening. "Then my time has come."

Next night Cat walked through the Wet Wild Woods and hid very near the Cave till morning-time, and Man and Dog and Horse went hunting. The Woman was busy cooking that morning, and the

Baby cried and interrupted. So she carried him outside the Cave and gave him a handful of pebbles to play with. But still the Baby cried.

Then the Cat put out his paddy paw and patted the Baby on the cheek, and it cooed; and the Cat rubbed against its fat knees and tickled it under its fat chin with his tail. And the Baby laughed; and the Woman heard him and smiled.

Then the Bat – the little upside-down Bat – that hung in the mouth of the Cave said, "O my Hostess and Wife of my Host and Mother of my Host's Son, a Wild Thing from the Wild Woods is most beautifully playing with your Baby."

"A blessing on that Wild Thing whoever he may be," said the Woman, straightening her back, "for I was a busy woman this morning and he has done me a service."

That very minute and second, the dried horse-skin Curtain that was stretched tail-down at the mouth of the Cave fell down – *woosh!* – because it remembered the bargain she had made with the Cat; and when the Woman went to pick it up – lo and behold! – the Cat was sitting quite comfy inside the Cave.

"O my Enemy and Wife of my Enemy and Mother of my Enemy," said the Cat, "it is I: for you have spoken a word in my praise, and now I can sit within the Cave for always and always. But still I am the Cat who walks by himself, and all places are alike to me."

The Woman was very angry, and shut her lips tight and took up her spinning-wheel and began to spin.

But the Baby cried because the Cat had gone away, and the Woman could not hush it, for it struggled and kicked and grew black in the face.

"O my Enemy and Wife of my Enemy and Mother of my Enemy," said the Cat, "take a strand of the thread that you are spinning and tie it to your spindle-whorl and drag it along the floor, and I will show you a magic that shall make your Baby laugh as loudly as he is now crying."

"I will do so," said the Woman, "because I am at my wits' end; but I will not thank you for it."

She tied the thread to the little clay spindle-whorl and drew it across the floor, and the Cat ran after it and patted it with his paws and rolled head over heels, and tossed it backward over his shoulder and chased it between his hind legs and pretended to lose it and pounced down upon it again, till the Baby laughed as loudly as it had been crying, and scrambled after the Cat and frolicked all over the Cave till it grew tired and settled down to sleep with the Cat in its arms.

"Now," said the Cat, "I will sing the Baby a song that shall keep him asleep for an hour." And he began to purr, loud and low, low and loud, till the Baby fell fast asleep. The Woman smiled as she looked down upon the two of them, and said, "That was wonderfully done. No question but you are very clever, O Cat."

That very minute and second, the smoke of the Fire at the back of the Cave came down in clouds from the roof – *puff!* – because it remembered the

Q. Where do cats come from?
A. *Catford; and Catterick.*

6

Q. What do you get if you cross a hyena with a cat?

A. *A giggle-puss.*

bargain she had made with the Cat; and when it had cleared away – lo and behold! – the Cat was sitting quite comfy close to the fire.

"O my Enemy and Wife of my Enemy and Mother of my Enemy," said the Cat, "it is I: for you have spoken a second word in my praise, and now I can sit by the warm fire at the back of the Cave for always and always and always. But still I am the Cat who walks by himself, and all places are alike to me."

Then the Woman was very very angry, and let down her hair and put more wood on the fire and brought out the broad blade-bone of the shoulder of mutton and began to make a Magic that should prevent her from saying a third word in praise of the Cat. It was not a Singing Magic, it was a Still Magic; and by and by the Cave grew so still that a little wee-wee mouse crept out of a corner and ran across the floor.

Q. What do you get if you cross a lemon with a cat?

A. *A sour-puss.*

"O my Enemy and Wife of my Enemy and Mother of my Enemy," said the Cat, "is that little mouse part of your Magic?"

"Ouh! Chee! No indeed!" said the Woman, and she dropped the blade-bone and jumped upon the footstool in front of the Fire and braided up her hair very quick for fear that the mouse should run up it.

"Ah!" said the Cat, watching. "Then the mouse will do me no harm if I eat it?"

"No," said the Woman, braiding up her hair, "eat it quickly and I will ever be grateful to you."

Cat made one jump and caught the little mouse, and the Woman said, "A hundred thanks. Even the First Friend is not quick enough to catch little mice as you have done. You must be very wise."

That very minute and second, the Milk-pot that stood by the fire cracked in two pieces – *ffft!* – because it remembered the bargain she had made

Q. What swims in the sea, and purrs?
A. *A cat-fish.*

Q. What cat has eight arms and lives in the sea?
A. *An octo-puss.*

Q. What do you get if you cross a tree with a cat?
A. *A pussy willow.*

Q. What has a head like a cat, feet like a cat,
   and a tail like a cat – but isn't?
A. *A kitten.*

with the Cat; and when the Woman jumped down
from the footstool – lo and behold! – the Cat was
lapping up the warm white milk that lay in one of
the broken pieces.

"O my Enemy and Wife of my Enemy and Mother
of my Enemy," said the Cat, "it is I: for you have
spoken three words in my praise, and now I can
drink the warm white milk three times a day for
always and always and always. But *still* I am the Cat
who walks by himself, and all places are alike to me."

Q. What do you get if you cross an ostrich with
   a cat?
A. *An emew.*

Cat

The fat cat on the mat
may seem to dream
of nice mice that suffice
for him, or cream;
but he is free, maybe,
walks in thought
unbowed, proud, where loud
roared and fought
his kin, lean and slim
or deep in den
in the East feasted on beasts
and tender men.

The giant lion with iron
claw in paw,
and huge ruthless tooth
in gory jaw;
the pard dark-starred
fleet upon feet,
that oft soft from aloft
leaps on his meat
where words loom in gloom –
for now they be
fierce and free,
and tamed is he;
but fat cat on the mat
kept as a pet
he does not forget.

J. R. R. Tolkien

2

CAT-CALLS
AND CAT-ERWAULS

According to experts, cats have at least sixteen different cat-noises to "talk" with. They murmur, squeak, cry out for food and attention, and have a jolly good sing-song on the tiles at night!

The most talkative cat is the Siamese, which has a wide range of different calls, and sometimes sounds like a baby crying.

Only the big cats have a special kind of throat that makes them roar.

Until very recently, no one knew exactly how cats purr. It has nothing to do with miaowing, since they can purr and mew at the same time! They seem to use a special part of the voice box. The bigger and older the cat, the more it will purr! It doesn't mean they love you more! Nobody really knows why cats purr, since they don't only do it when they are contented.

How cats got their purr is told in a story about a princess. She was forced to spin 10,000 lengths of linen thread within thirty days in order to save her true love from death. She got her three cats to help her, and their reward was their purr – like the sound of a spinning-wheel!

This cat's an opera singer
She likes a nightly tune
She dresses up in shadows
And serenades the moon.

Sally Kindberg

Hey diddle diddle,
The cat and the fiddle,
The cow jumped over the moon;
The little dog laughed to see such sport,
And the dish ran away with the spoon.

When cats get up in the morning,
They always say Good day,
When cats get up in the morning,
They always say Good day,
Miaow! Miaow! Miaow! Miaow!
That is what they say,
They say, Miaow! Miaow!
Miaow! Miaow! That is what they say.

There was a young curate of Kew,
Who kept a tom cat in a pew;
He taught it to speak
Alphabetical Greek,
But it never got further than μ [mew].

Q. What do you get if you cross a cat with a
    hammer and a saw?
A. *A tool kitty.*

Puss came dancing out of the barn
With a pair of bagpipes under her arm;
She could play nothing but "Fiddle cum fee,
The fly has married the bumble-bee".
Then all the birds of the air did sing,
"Did ever you hear so merry a thing?"
Fiddle cum fee, fiddle cum fee,
The fly has married the bumble-bee!

The Owl and the Pussy Cat

The Owl and the Pussy Cat went to sea
In a beautiful pea-green boat.
They took some honey, and plenty of money,
Wrapped up in a five-pound note.
The Owl looked up to the stars above,
And sang to a small guitar,
"O lovely Pussy! O Pussy, my love,
What a beautiful Pussy you are,
You are,
You are!
What a beautiful Pussy you are!"

Pussy said to the Owl, "You elegant fowl!
How charmingly sweet you sing!
O let us be married! Too long we have tarried:
But what shall we do for a ring?"
They sailed away, for a year and a day,
To the land where the Bong-tree grows,
And there in a wood a Piggy-wig stood
With a ring at the end of his nose,
His nose,
His nose,
With a ring at the end of his nose.

"Dear Pig, are you willing to sell for one shilling
Your ring?" Said the Piggy, "I will."
So they took it away, and were married next day
By the Turkey who lives on the hill.
They dined on mince, and slices of quince,
Which they ate with a runcible spoon;
And hand in hand, on the edge of the sand,
They danced by the light of the moon,
The moon,
The moon,
They danced by the light of the moon.

Edward Lear

How The Cat Became

by Ted Hughes

Things were running very smoothly and most of the creatures were highly pleased with themselves. Lion was already famous. Even the little shrews and moles and spiders were pretty well known.

But among all these busy creatures there was one who seemed to be getting nowhere. It was Cat.

Cat was a real oddity. The others didn't know what to make of him at all.

He lived in a hollow tree in the wood. Every night, when the rest of the creatures were sound asleep, he retired to the depths of his tree – then such sounds, such screechings, yowlings, wailings! The bats that slept upside-down all day long in the hollows of the tree branches awoke with a start and fled with their wing-tips stuffed into their ears. It seemed to them that Cat was having the worst nightmares ever – ten at a time.

But no. Cat was tuning his violin.

If only you could have seen him! Curled in the warm smooth hollow of his tree, gazing up through the hole at the top of the trunk, smiling at the stars, winking at the moon – his violin tucked under his chin. Ah, Cat was a happy one.

And all night long he sat there composing his tunes.

Q. What do cats try for?
A. *Purr-fection!*

Now the creatures didn't like this at all. They saw no use in his music, it made no food, it built no nest, it didn't even keep him warm. And the way Cat lounged around all day, sleeping in the sun, was just more than they could stand.

"He's a bad example," said Beaver. "He never does a stroke of work! What if our children think they can live as idly as he does?"

"It's time," said Weasel, "that Cat had a job like everybody else in the world."

So the creatures of the wood formed a Committee to persuade Cat to take a job.

Q. Why does a cat purr.
A. *Because it has a purr-puss (purpose).*

Jay, Magpie and Parrot went along at dawn and sat in the topmost twigs of Cat's old tree. As soon as Cat poked his head out, they all began together:

"You've got to get a job. Get a job! Get a job!"

That was only the beginning of it. All day long, everywhere he went, those birds were at him:

"Get a job! Get a job!"

And try as he would, Cat could not get one wink of sleep.

That night he went back to his tree early. He was far too tired to practise on his violin and fell fast asleep in a few minutes. Next morning, when he poked his head out of the tree at first light, the three birds of the Committee were there again, loud as ever:

"Get a job!"

Cat ducked back down into his tree and began to think. He wasn't going to start grubbing around in the wet woods all day, as they wanted him to. Oh, no. He wouldn't have any time to play his violin if he did that. There was only one thing to do and he did it.

He tucked his violin under his arm and suddenly jumped out at the top of the tree and set off through the woods at a run. Behind him, shouting and calling, came Jay, Magpie and Parrot.

Q. What sounds worse than a cat stuck in a tree?
A. *Two cats stuck in a tree!*

Other creatures that were about their daily work in the undergrowth looked up when Cat ran past. No one had ever seen Cat run before.

"Cat's up to something," they called to each other. "Maybe he's going to get a job at last."

Deer, Wild Boar, Bear, Ferret, Mongoose, Porcupine and a cloud of birds set off after Cat to see where he was going.

After a great deal of running they came to the edge of the forest. There they stopped. As they peered through the leaves they looked sideways at each other and trembled. Ahead of them, across an open field covered with haycocks, was Man's farm.

But Cat wasn't afraid. He went straight on, over the field, and up to Man's door. He raised his paw and banged as hard as he could in the middle of the door.

Man was so surprised to see Cat that at first he just stood, eyes wide, mouth open. No creature ever dared to come on to his fields, let alone knock at his door. Cat spoke first.

"I've come for a job," he said.

"A job?" asked Man, hardly able to believe his ears.

"Work," said Cat. "I want to earn my living."

Man looked him up and down, then saw his long claws.

"You look as if you'd make a fine rat-catcher," said Man.

Cat was surprised to hear that. He wondered what it was about him that made him look like a rat-catcher. Still, he wasn't going to miss the chance of a job. So he stuck out his chest and said: "Been doing it for years."

Q. What do cats like to read?
A. *The* Mews of the World.

Customer: "Have you any cats going cheap?"

Pet-shop Owner: "Sorry, all our cats go miaow!"

"Well then, I've a job for you," said Man. "My farm's swarming with rats and mice. They're in my haystacks, they're in my corn sacks, and they're all over the pantry."

So before Cat knew where he was, he had been signed on as a rat-and-mouse-catcher. His pay was milk and meat, and a place at the fireside. He slept all day and worked all night.

At first he had a terrible time. The rats pulled his tail, the mice nipped his ears. They climbed on to rafters above him and dropped down – *thump!* – on to him in the dark. They teased the life out of him.

But Cat was a quick learner. At the end of the week he could lay out a dozen rats and twice as many mice within half an hour. If he'd gone on laying them out all night there would pretty soon have

Q. What does a two-ton mouse say?
A. *"Here, kitty, kitty . . ."*

Q. What kind of car do cats like?
A. *A Purr-geot.*

been none left, and Cat would have been out of a job. So he caught a few each night – in the first ten minutes or so. Then he retired into the barn and played his violin till morning. This was just the job he had been looking for.

Man was delighted with him. And Mrs Man thought he was beautiful. She took him on to her lap and stroked him for hours on end. What a life! thought Cat. If only those silly creatures in the dripping wet woods could see him now!

Q. How does a cat go up the M1?
A. *Meeeeeeeeeeoooooooowwww!*

Q. What do cats like to do in their spare time?
A. *Play mewsic.*

Well, when the other farmers saw what a fine rat-and-mouse-catcher Cat was, they all wanted cats too. Soon there were so many cats that our Cat decided to form a string band. Oh yes, they were all great violinists. Every night, after making one pile of rats and another of mice, each cat left his farm and was away over the fields to a little dark spinney.

Then what tunes! All night long . . .

Pretty soon lady cats began to arrive. Now, every night, instead of just music, there was dancing too. And what dances! If only you could have crept up there and peeped into the glade from behind a tree

Q. What did the cat say to the budgie?
A. *"Miaow. Miaow."*

and seen the cats dancing – the glossy furred ladies and the tom cats, some pearly grey, some ginger red, and all with wonderful green flashing eyes. Up and down the glade, with the music flying out all over the night.

At dawn they hung their violins in the larch trees, dashed back to the farms, and pretended they had been working all night among the rats and mice. They lapped their milk hungrily, stretched out at the fireside, and fell asleep with smiles on their faces.

Q. Where do cats go when they die?
A. *To purr-gatory.*

Q. What do cats like for dessert?
A. *Strawberry mouse.*

3

CATS AT WORK

The Egyptians seem to have been the first to domesticate the wild cats, about 5000 years ago; but they didn't really have them as pets. Their cats had to work for their keep, as they did in China and Japan, and as many still do, of course: catching birds and guarding the grain stores from mice. There's a painting of a cat with a collar round its neck in a tomb dated 2600 BC – that's more than 4500 years ago. But the Egyptians liked their cats very much: they let them eat from their plates, and when one died its owner shaved his eyebrows as a sign of his sorrow! No one was supposed to kill a cat. There were probably about a hundred thousand cats in Alexandria alone! The name for the cat in ancient Egypt was *myeo* or *miu* – where our words "miaow" and "mew" come from.

Cats were believed to have been brought to Britain by a descendant of the daughter of one of the Pharaohs. There are no records of any cats in Europe until the first century AD. The Phoenicians and then the Romans are most likely to have actually brought cats to Britain: the Phoenicians through trading, and the Romans when they came to conquer Britain and build towns and villas. Cat bones have been found in the remains of a Roman villa at Lullingstone in Kent.

Although cats through the ages were valued for their mouse-catching by farmers, millers, brewers and monks, they weren't really wanted as pets until the eighteenth and nineteenth centuries. Many people were actually afraid of them in the Middle Ages, and thought of them only as the companions of witches. If people had liked cats better, then there might have been no Great Plague of London in 1665: there weren't enough cats around to catch all the rats, which were the carriers of the plague germs.

The Home Office employs a working cat to catch mice, and has done since 1883. The cat is always called Peter! Cats also work in post offices, warehouses, hotels, railway stations, theatres, libraries and on board ship. There are six cats in the British Museum, which are paid £500 a year for their board and lodging to catch mice.

Q. What kind of cat do you find in a library?
A. *A cat-alogue.*

There are some good champion mousers and rat-
ters: Towser, in a Perthshire distillery, caught at least
three mice a day over twenty-three years from 1963;
Minnie caught nearly 12,500 rats in six years at the
White City Stadium, from 1927–33. A cat named
Wilberforce worked at 10 Downing Street for eighteen years until he retired. He saw four Prime Minis-
ters: Edward Heath, Harold Wilson, James
Callaghan, and Margaret Thatcher. The most famous
station cat must be Tiddles at Paddington, who grew
very fat from gifts from friendly commuters in the
1970s, and who lived in the ladies' cloakroom on
Platform One.

Two Little Kittens

Two little kittens, one stormy night,
Began to quarrel and then to fight;
One had a mouse, the other had none,
And that was the way the quarrel began.

"I'll have that mouse!" said the bigger cat;
"You'll have that mouse? We'll see about that."
"I will have that mouse," said the elder one;
"You shan't have that mouse," said the little one.

I told you before 'twas a stormy night
When these two little kittens began to fight;
The old woman seized her sweeping broom
And swept the two kittens right out of the room.

Patient: "Doctor, doctor, my husband thinks he's
    a cat."
Doctor: "Then bring him here for treatment."
Patient: "No thank you – who would catch all the
    mice?"

The ground was covered with frost and snow,
And the two little kittens had nowhere to go;
So they laid them down on the mat at the door,
While the angry old woman was sweeping the floor.

And then they crept in as quiet as mice,
All wet with snow and as cold as ice,
For they found it was better, that stormy night,
To lie down and sleep than to quarrel and fight.

Four little mice sat down to spin;
Pussy passed by and she peeped in.
  "What are you doing, my little men?"
  "Weaving coats for gentlemen."
    "Shall I come in and cut off your threads?"
    "No, no, Mistress Pussy, you'd bite off our heads."
      "Oh, no, I'll not; I'll help you to spin."
      "That may be so, but you don't come in."

Not last night but the night before
Two tom cats came knocking at my door.
I went downstairs to let them in
They knocked me down with a rolling pin.

Pussy cat, pussy cat, where have you been?
I've been to London to look at the Queen.
Pussy cat, pussy cat, what did you there?
I frightened a little mouse under the chair.

Pussy Cat, Pussy Cat

Pussy cat, pussy cat, where have you been,
Licking your lips with your whiskers so clean?
Pussy cat, pussy cat, purring and pudgy,
Pussy cat, pussy cat, WHERE IS OUR BUDGIE?

Max Fatchen

American Cat in London

Dressed smartly in his fur coat,
The cat is a businessman,
With no guarantee.
The Cat,
With his gas mask face,
Is a dirty dealer.
Cat Capone is back in town.

The Cat,
Carried away with its short-comings,
Arrested,
Charged,
Imprisoned.

Bail paid and cat walks free.
Cat's eyes stab the dark,
As he strides out of his house,
His coat almost merged into the Victorian
Bricks of the terrace.
His whiskers a moustache,
His claws
Are his pens,
And his mouth, his briefcase.

This cat's ears are Sky Television receivers,
As used by his next door neighbour.
The cat is a cat burglar no more.
Yes, the cat is a businessman,
In a big bad back yard.

James Noble

4
CATS AT HOME

Queen Victoria did a lot to make cats popular as pets. She liked them very much, and asked the RSPCA when it was founded in 1824 to make sure that a cat was put on the Queen's Medal for the society. The first Cat Show was held at Crystal Palace in 1871, with 170 cats. Another person who helped to popularize cats was an artist called Louis Wain, who was very fond of his own black and white cat called Peter. For thirty years, until the First World War, he drew thousands and thousands of comic cats for postcards, annuals, pop-up books and ornaments. Most of his cat pictures showed them dressed and walking like people. In 1890 he was made president of the National Cat Club. He was a very eccentric man, with some strange ideas, but he was right when he said that people would be healthier and would live longer if they had a cat, because their lives would be less stressful.

Nowadays, there are nearly seven million pet cats in Britain, in four and a half million homes: soon to catch up with the dog as favourite pet (nearly seven and a half million). That means 1250 tons of pet food between them! And 9 out of 10 cats do really seem to prefer Whiskas . . . Ninety per cent of all cat owners give their cats tinned food rather than fresh food at least once a week. In the 1980s there were estimated to be over 50 million cats in the USA! More food is bought there for cats than for people. Just think how many tons of cat litter they all need!

There are about a hundred breeds of pedigree cats, but they are basically either long-haired (like the Angora and Persian) or short-haired (like the Siamese and the Abyssinian). Our most popular cat is the cross-breed or "moggie" with a tabby, or blotchy patterned fur; the Siamese is the most popular pedigree, brought to England only in 1886. Much revered in Siam, legend has it that they got their "cross eyes" from staring too long at the golden goblet of Buddha. In the Scottish islands there are lots of tortoiseshell and marmalade cats, brought there probably by Viking settlers. Everyone knows the Manx cat, which has no tail, but no one knows how it got to the Isle of Man. One story says it came with the Spanish Armada from the Middle East; another that it arrived so late at Noah's Ark that Noah accidentally shut the door on its tail!

Q. How does a cat feel when it has got rid of all the mice?
A. *Mouse-proud.*

The smallest domestic cat seems to be the "drain-cat" from Singapore, which does like drains, and which weighs only 1.8–2.7 kg (the average weight of a cat is between 2 and 5 kg); the largest is the American "Ragdoll", which weighs three times the average, and gets its name from looking like a limp doll when it is carried. Other unusual breeds include the hairless "Sphynx", the "Rex" with a woolly coat, and the "Scottish Fold" with droopy ears!

At home we sit and drink our tea
Or maybe toast a mouse.
We don't like vegetarians
Calling at our house.

Sally Kindberg

My cat is kind in winter
He climbs up on my head
And then he warms my feet at night
By lying on my bed.

Sally Kindberg

A Siamese kitten called Ming
Liked to play with long pieces of string.
One day, finding a ball,
She unravelled it all,
And it stretched from East Grinstead to Tring.

There was a young lady named Pat
Who had just bought a very good cat.
She then bought it a mouse,
Who lived in the house,
And sometimes they all had a chat.

Q. What does a cat rest its head on when it goes
   to sleep?
A. *A cat-erpillar.*

Q. What do cats like to eat at the cinema?
A. *Choc-mice.*

Rat a tat tat, who is that?
Only Grandma's pussy cat.
What do you want?
A pint of milk.
Where's your money?
In my pocket.
Where's your pocket?
I forgot it.
Oh, you silly pussy cat!

Squatter's Rights

Listen, kitten,
Get this clear;
This is my chair,
I sit here.

Okay, kitty,
We can share;
When I'm not home,
It's your chair.

Listen tom cat,
How about
If I use it
When you're out?

Richard Shaw

This is My Chair

This is my chair.
Go away and sit somewhere else.
This one is all my own.
It is the only thing in your house that I possess
And insist upon possessing.
Everything else therein is yours.
My dish,
My toys,
My basket,
My scratching post and my ping-pong ball;
You provided them for me.
This chair I selected for myself.
I like it.
It suits me.
You have the sofa,
The stuffed chair
And the footstool.
I don't go and sit on them, do I?
Then why cannot you leave me mine,
And let us have no further argument.

Paul Gallico

Q. What happened to the cat who swallowed
   some wool?
A. *She had mittens.*

Why Do Cats Wash After Eating?

You may have noticed, little friends,
That cats don't wash their faces
Before they eat, as children do,
In all good Christian places.

Well, years ago, a famous cat,
The pangs of hunger feeling,
Had chanced to catch a fine young mouse,
Who said, as he ceased squealing:

"All genteel folk their faces wash
Before they think of eating."
And, wishing to be thought well bred,
Puss heeded his entreating.

But when she raised her paw to wash,
Chance for escape affording,
The sly young mouse said his goodbye,
Without respect to wording.

A feline counsel met that day,
And passed in solemn meeting,
A law, forbidding any cat
To wash till after eating.

According to another legend, a cat one day caught a sparrow, and was just about to eat it when the sparrow said, "No gentleman eats until he has washed his face." The cat was very upset by this, so he put the sparrow down to wash his face with his paw. Of course, the sparrow flew away! The cat said, "As long as I live I will eat first and *then* wash my face!"

Q. What do you get if you cross a Chinese cat with an alley cat?
A. *A Peking Tom.*

Rindle, Randle
Light the candle,
The cat's among the pies;
No matter for that,
The cat'll get fat,
And I'm too lazy to rise.

Patient: "Doctor, doctor. I think I'm a cat."
Doctor: "When did this start?"
Patient: "When I was a kitten."

Three Little Kittens

Three little kittens, they lost their mittens,
And they began to cry,
"Oh, mammy dear,
We sadly fear
Our mittens we have lost!"
"What! Lost your mittens, you naughty kittens,
Then you shall have no pie."

Three little kittens, they found their mittens,
And they began to cry,
"Oh, mammy dear,
See here, see here,
Our mittens we have found."
"What? Found your mittens, you good little kittens,
Then you shall have some pie."

Pussy cat mew jumped over a coal,
And in her best petticoat
Burnt a great hole;
Pussy cat mew shall have no more milk,
Till her best petticoat's mended with silk.

The three little kittens put on their mittens,
And soon ate up the pie;
"Oh, mammy dear,
We greatly fear
Our mittens we have soiled."
"What! Soiled your mittens, you naughty kittens!"
Then they began to sigh.

The three little kittens, they washed their mittens,
And hung them up to dry;
"Oh, mammy dear,
Look here, look here,
Our mittens we have washed."
"What! Washed your mittens, you darling kittens!
But I smell a rat close by!"

Pussy cat, wussy cat, with a white foot,
When is your wedding and I'll come to it.
The beer's to brew, the bread's to bake.
Pussy cat, pussy cat, don't be late.

Under-The-Table-Manners

It's very hard to be polite
If you're a cat.
When other folks are up at table
Eating all that they are able,
You are down upon the mat
If you're a cat.

You're expected just to sit
If you're a cat.
Not to let them know you're there
By scratching on the chair,
Or a light, respected pat
If you're a cat.

You are not to make a fuss
If you're a cat.
Tho' there's fish upon the plate,
You're expected just to wait,
Wait politely on the mat
If you're a cat.

Cat Poem

You're black and sleek and beautiful
What a pity your best friends won't tell you
Your breath smells of Kit-E-Kat.

Adrian Henri

Quick, quick
The cat's been sick.
Where, where?
Under the chair.
Hasten, hasten
Fetch the basin.

Q. What do cats like to eat for breakfast?
A. *Mice Krispies.*

Conversation on a Garden Wall

Move over, you've got all the bricks with the sun on.
   Oh, all right. Mind you, I was here first.

He came round after me again last night. Right up
to the back door.
   Really? He's persistent, I'll say that for him.
I'll say. Anyway, they chased him away.

How are yours treating you?

Not too bad, really. They're a bit careful with the milk.

> *Oh, mine are all right about that. They're a bit unimaginative with my food, though. Last week I had the same meal every day.*

You don't say. The food's OK. It's a real pain being pushed out in the rain. Every night, rain or snow, out I go.

> *Me, too. Look, he is back again.*

Cheek. Pretend to take no notice.

> *At least you've got a quiet place with none of those small ones around. I hardly get a minute.*

That's true. All mine do is sit in front of a little box with tiny ones inside it.

> *Mine do too. It's the only peace I get.*

And one of them pushes that noisy thing round the floor every day.

> *Terrible, isn't it? Mind you, mine only does it once or twice a week.*

You're lucky. Oh, the sun's gone in.

> *Yes, time for a stroll. I'll jump down and just sort of walk past him, accidentally.*

Accidentally on purpose, you mean. See you around.

> *Yes, see you around. I'll tell you one thing, though.*

What's that?

> *It's a good job they can't talk, isn't it?*

Adrian Henri

The Tortoiseshell Cat

The tortoiseshell cat
She sits on the mat
As gay as a sunflower she;
In orange and black you see her blink,
And her waistcoat's white, and her nose is pink,
And her eyes are green of the sea.
But all is vanity, all the way;
Twilight's coming, and close of day,
And every cat in the twilight's grey,
Every possible cat.

Patrick Chalmers

Q. Why was the cat so small?
A. *It was brought up on condensed milk.*

5

A CAT-ALOGUE
OF NAMES

According to a survey by Spillers Catfoods, the most popular name for British pussy cats is Sooty – no prizes for guessing the cat's colour! This is followed by Smokey, Brandy and Fluffy. Other popular names include Tiger, Tigger, Kitty, Whisky, Sylvester, Tom and Willum. Sylvester and Tom, of course, are very popular cartoon cats, chasing Tweetie Pie the canary and Jerry the mouse.

What is your cat called? Has it got an unusual name? Like Seraphim, Japonica or Lydia La Poose? The nineteenth-century poet Samuel Taylor Coleridge called his cat The Most Noble The Archduke Rumperstilschen, Marcus Macbum, Earl Tomnefuagne, Baron Raticide, Waowhler and Scratch: or Rumpel for short! Champion pedigree cats usually have very exotic names, like Moonstruck Lylac Tyger, Snowfleet Firefly. Mousepolice Charlie sounds quite fun, and Headway Rambo is probably very big!

Witches' cats were popularly called Grimalkin or Graymalkin, from a word meaning "devil". You can read about witches' cats elsewhere in this book.

Q. Where do cats like to live?
A. *In a Mews.*

Choosing their Names

Our old cat has kittens three –
What do you think their names should be?

One is tabby with emerald eyes,
And a tail that's long and slender,
And into a temper she quickly flies
If you ever by chance offend her.
I think we shall call her this –
I think we shall call her that –
Now don't you think that Pepperpot
Is a nice name for a cat?

One is black with a frill of white,
And her feet are all white fur,
If you stroke her she carries her tail upright
And quickly begins to purr.
I think we shall call her this –
I think we shall call her that –
Now don't you think that Sootikin
Is a nice name for a cat?

One is a tortoiseshell yellow and black,
With plenty of white about him;
If you tease him, at once he sets up his back,
He's a quarrelsome one, ne'er doubt him.
I think we shall call him this –
I think we shall call him that –
Now don't you think that Scratchaway
Is a nice name for a cat?

Thomas Hood

Q. Where do cats like to go for their holidays?
A. *Katmandu; and also the Canary Islands.*

Our kitten, the one we call Louie,
Will never eat liver so chewy,
Nor the milk, nor the fish
That we put in his dish.
He only will dine on chop suey.

Q. What do cats say to each other at Christmas?
A. *"A Merry Christmouse and a Happy Mew Year!"*

My Cat

Can you draw a picture of your cat here?
Look at some of the ways people describe their cats
on the next page.
How would you describe your cat?

Cat Colours and Patterns
(some of them)

sable	mackerel
champagne	lavender
platinum	spotted
mink	blotched
leopard	honey mink
rosetted	blue grey
single spotted	golden agouti
black-tortie-smoke	blue tabby
sepia silver	ruddy
jet black	fawn
mahogany	blue patched tabby
chocolate point	ash grey
harlequin	slate grey
cream	chinchilla
caramel	tortoiseshell
apricot	tipped
black smoke	ghost tabby
indigo	blue cream
chalky white	bronze
black silver	black shaded silver
seal	blue golden
lilac	chocolate golden
red	lilac golden
auburn	warm ivory
sorrel	unbleached muslin
cinnamon	calico

Q. Where do cats keep their money?
A. *In a kitty.*

Q. Where do cats keep their clothes?
A. *In a kit-bag.*

Q. Who do cats get their Christmas presents from?
A. *Santa Claws.*

Q. What do you call a cat that has swallowed a duck?
A. *A duck-filled fatty puss.*

Q. What do you call a cat in the chemist's?
A. *Puss in Boots.*

6

CAT LOVERS

Believe it or not, there are people who don't like cats at all, or who are really terrified of them! It seems strange that this applies to some of the most famous soldiers and dictators in history: like Alexander the Great, Genghis Khan, Julius Caesar, Napoleon Bonaparte, Earl Kitchener, Mussolini and Adolf Hitler. President Eisenhower didn't like cats very much, and nor did the composer Brahms: he used to shoot at them with a bow and arrow.

Some people are allergic to cats, and sneeze and cough when they are near them. James Boswell, the biographer of Dr Samuel Johnson, was one. The President of the United States, Bill Clinton, is allergic to his daughter Chelsea's cat called Socks. Perhaps one day Socks will have his story published, like President Roosevelt's cat Tom Quartz and President Bush's spaniel Millie!

Florence Nightingale, however, liked cats so much, she had sixty of them! They all had names of politicians, like Disraeli, Gladstone and Bismarck. The American writer Ernest Hemingway had forty cats, and the poet Lord Byron had five, as well as ten horses, eight dogs and an eagle! The philosopher and economist Jeremy Bentham had his cat "knighted": it was called the Reverend Doctor Sir John Langborn. He also fed it on macaroni! The comic poet Edward Lear was so besotted with his cat Foss that he didn't want to upset him when he moved house, so that he had his new house built exactly like the old one! The prophet Mohammed was also very considerate: he is said to have cut off the hem of the long sleeve of his cloak before getting up, so that he would not disturb his cat Muezza, who had fallen asleep on it. Rather than disturb his pet cat Sizi, who liked to sleep on his arm, Albert Schweitzer would write with his other hand. The Earl of Southampton's cat was so attached to him that it came to find him in the Tower, and kept him company during his last hours.

Many famous writers have worked with cats close by or lying on their shoulders: Henry James, John Keats, Matthew Arnold, Sir Walter Scott, Edgar Allan Poe, Thomas Hardy and Raymond Chandler. Dr Samuel Johnson fed his cat Hodge on oysters! The Italian poet Dante's cat is supposed to have held a candle between its paws so that Dante could see to write! T. S. Eliot, Beatrix Potter, Mark Twain and the French poet Charles Baudelaire all wrote cats into their work. Other cats have shared state secrets: Cardinal Wolsey's, Cardinal Richelieu's, Pope Leo XII's and Sir Winston Churchill's cat Nelson. Today, famous personalities like Phil Collins, Brigitte Bardot, Rolf Harris, Bobby Moore and Princess Michael of Kent, are all cat lovers.

Do you know what famous cat lover invented the cat-flap? It was the scientist Sir Isaac Newton (1642–1727)! He had two holes made in his door, one for his cat and one for her kittens.

Said a miserly peer at the Abbey,
"I fear I shall look rather shabby,
For I've replaced my ermine,
Infested with vermin,
With the fur of my dear defunct tabby."

There was an Old Man on the Border,
Who lived in the utmost disorder;
He danced with the Cat,
And made Tea in his Hat,
Which vexed all the folks on the Border.

Edward Lear

Pangur Ban

I and Pangur Ban, my cat,
'Tis a like task we are at;
Hunting mice is his delight,
Hunting words I sit all night.

Better far than praise of men
'Tis to sit with book and pen;
Pangur bears me no ill will,
He too plies his simple skill.

'Tis a merry thing to see
At our tasks how glad are we.
When at home we sit and find
Entertainment to our mind.

Oftentimes a mouse will stray
In the hero Pangur's way;
Oftentimes my keen thought set
Takes a meaning in its net.

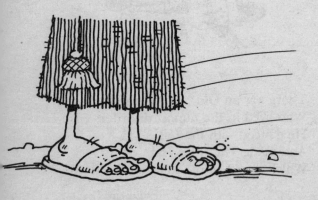

'Gainst the wall he sets his eye
Full and fierce and sharp and sly;
'Gainst the wall of knowledge I
All my little wisdom try.

When a mouse darts from its den,
O how glad is Pangur then!
O what gladness do I prove
When I solve the doubts I love!

So in peace our tasks we ply,
Pangur Ban, my cat and I;
In our hearts we find our bliss,
I have mine and he has his.

Practice every day has made
Pangur perfect in his trade;
I get wisdom day and night
Turning darkness into light.

Irish, ninth-century.
Translation by Robin Flower

I love little pussy,
Her coat is so warm,
And if I don't hurt her,
She'll do me no harm.
So I'll not pull her tail,
Nor drive her away,
But puss and I
Very gently will play.

I'll pat pretty pussy,
And then she will purr;
And thus show her thanks
For my kindness to her.
But I'll not pinch her ears,
Nor tread on her paw,
Lest I should provoke her
To use her sharp claw.
I never will vex her
Nor make her displeased –
For pussy don't like to be worried and teased.

My Kitten

I have a whiskery kitten
With big round eyes
That are always wide and shiny
And full of surprise.

And when I dress each morning
In difficult clothes,
She gently reaches out a paw
To pat my toes.

Leila Berg

7

PAWS

FOR THOUGHT . . .

Cats' eyes are wonderful. In very strong light, their eyes close to slits, in very dim light they are rounder. This is because they are used to hunting at night. Cats also have stereoscopic vision! Each eye sees a different angle of view, then they combine to form an impression of depth and solidity. And they can see through an angle of 205 degrees. But they are really colour-blind. They have a third eye-lid which closes upwards when they are unwell, or in deep undergrowth. The colour of their eyes can be orange, yellow, green, hazel, pale blue or dark blue.

Cats also have good hearing. They can hear up to 60,000 or more cycles, and more than a dog can, whereas a human being hears only up to 20,000 (the top note of a violin). That's why cats can hear mice squeaking!

Cats have lots of teeth (28 to 30), and five claws on each front paw, four on the back paw, which they draw back into their paws when they don't need to use them.

The cat's tongue is very rough so that it is like a comb, to keep its fur very clean. And the saliva is like soap-powder, a special cleaning fluid!

They really are the cats' whiskers! These are very sensitive, like feelers, to help them in their hunting and moving about in difficult places, holes and gaps. Anywhere the head can go, the body can follow!

Cats really do like cat-naps! All cats, pet cats and wild cats, will often sleep for eighteen hours a day, especially as they get older. They spend two-thirds of their life asleep!

Cats are very good acrobats and gymnasts. They can jump up to five times their own height! They hardly ever misjudge distances. They nearly always land on their feet, if they jump off something, or fall. This is because they have a very flexible spine.

Cats usually live to between fourteen and twenty years old these days. The world record, held by a cat called Puss in Devon, stands at thirty-six. Today, the oldest cat in Britain is a Siamese called Sukoo, also from Devon! Aged thirty-four.

You might be surprised to know that cats like dogs better than cats like cats or dogs like dogs! They don't always fight like cats and dogs.

Did you know that a group of cats is called a "clowder"; and a litter of kittens is called a "kindle"? Sometimes just one kitten born in a litter is called a kindle as well. One tabby called Daisy had 420 kittens! (Not all at once.) The average litter is two to six kittens and all kittens are born blind. One Burmese cat once had a litter of nineteen kittens!

The word "caterpillar" does have something to do with cats! It comes from a Latin word meaning "cat-haired worm"!

In 1936 you could have gone cat-racing in Weymouth. The course was 200 metres long, and the cats chased an electric mouse! Cats can run very fast when they are scared. About twenty-five miles an hour!

Q. How are a cat and a comma different?

A. *A cat has claws at the end of its paws, and a comma has a pause at the end of its clause.*

Some pussies are very pampered. The richest cats in the world must be Hellcat and Brownie in California who were once left 415 million dollars in their owner's will. Another American cat, Charlie Chan, was left a three-bedroom house and an antiques collection! There is a pet motel in Illinois which offers apartments for cats, and in California cats have their own department store and dating service!

An old lady in Hereford has eleven cats in her house, but ten of them are stuffed! They are all called Timmy. Only one comes for tea when it is called!

8

CAT WORSHIP

It was the Egyptians, who first brought cats out of the wild into their dwellings to hunt for mice, and who liked them very much, who also seem to have been the first to worship cats as gods and goddesses. The lion-headed goddess of pleasure, Bast or Pasht, was worshipped from 1780 BC to AD 392, and was supposed to protect cats and people from evil spirits. She was also the protector of pregnant women. One story has it that Pasht is where our word "puss" comes from. But the word doesn't appear in English until the seventeenth century, so nobody is really sure about this.

Our modern use of eye-liner may come from the Egyptians, who had the cat-like eyes of Pasht as their model! The goddess's father turned into a cat at dawn, to drive away the night.

If a cat was killed, eternal darkness was threatened: Egypt went to war with Rome when a Roman soldier accidentally killed one! The war ended after the deaths of Antony and Cleopatra.

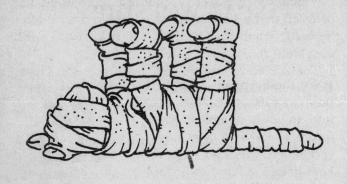

Mummified bodies of dead cats, and also mice for their food, have been found in excavations of many Egyptian tombs.

The Egyptians believed that cats' eyes caught the light of the sun by day, and reflected it back at night. Many legends all over the world link the cat to the sun; and also to the moon, because the pupils of cats' eyes grow big or small like the moon waxing and waning. Chinese and Roman children used to try to see the changes of the moon in their eyes. The ancient Greeks believed that when the world first began, the sun made the lion, and the moon made the cat. Some Americans believe that the moon wanes because it is being eaten by mice!

Some Buddhists, however, didn't think much of cats. The cat was the only animal that was not invited to Buddha's funeral, because when Buddha was ill, the cat ate the rat who had been bringing the medicine that would have cured him. Nor did the cat weep when Buddha died.

But in Siam and Thailand, Siamese and Burmese cats guarded the sacred Buddhist temples. It was believed that a holy man's spirit entered a cat after he died. When the cat died, the holy man's spirit then went to paradise.

There is also a temple dedicated to cats in Japan. All the cat statues there have their right paw raised, as if to say "hello". Little models of these cats can be bought today as teapots and souvenirs!

As we have already seen earlier, the prophet Mohammed, who lived in the seventh century, loved cats. Tabby cats are supposed to have the initial "M" on their foreheads, because of Mohammed. One story says that Mohammed was trying to write a sermon, but was disturbed by a mouse. A cat got rid of it for him, and when Mohammed stroked the cat's forehead to say thank you, the letter "M" appeared.

In the Islamic religion cats are more highly esteemed than dogs, and can enter the mosques, because they are thought to have souls. They are also believed to face Mecca when they wash themselves, like true Muslims do when they pray.

There are hardly any cats at all in the Bible. There were probably too many rumours flying around about cats being the servants of the devil when it was written! One biblical legend, however, tells how the cat came to be created. Noah's family complained about all the rats and mice eating the food on the Ark, so Noah stroked the lion to make him sneeze, and out came the cat from his nose!

Q. Who wrote *Thoughts of a Chinese Cat*?
A. *Chairman Miaow.*

Knock, knock.
Who's there?
Ammonia.
Ammonia who?
Ammonia a little cat who can't reach the cat-flap.

Another legend says that the moment Jesus Christ was born in Bethlehem, a cat under the manger gave him her kittens as a present.

Many saints loved cats, including St Yves, the patron of lawyers, and St Francis of Assisi, who loved all animals: St Patrick of Ireland, St Agatha, St Gertrude and Pope Gregory Magro were all cat fans.

Another story explains why cats like to sit in front of mouse-holes. They are waiting for two mice, out of hundreds, who escaped after they tormented St Francis by order of the devil. Because of stories like this, and because they were useful in catching mice anyway, cats were the only animals allowed in English nunneries in the Middle Ages.

Q. How is cat food sold?
A. *Purr can.*

St Jerome and His Lion

St Jerome in his study kept a great big cat,
It's always in his pictures, with its feet upon the mat.
Did he give it milk to drink, in a little dish?
When it came to Fridays did he give it fish?
If I lost my little cat, I'd be sad without it:
I should ask St Jeremy what to do about it:
I should ask St Jeremy, just because of that,
For he's only the only saint I know who kept a
pussy cat.

9

CATS, WITCHES
AND
BLACK MAGIC

There are not only good gods and goddesses, and sacred or holy cats, but also bad gods and goddesses, and cats linked with evil, the devil and black magic. The Romans had a goddess of the moon and darkness who was called Diana, who could change herself into a cat. Her brother was Lucifer, who had a magical cat which slept with him. Diana had a daughter who grew up to teach people witchcraft. The Greek goddess, Hecate, who was the same as the Roman goddess Diana, was often shown with a black cat.

In the Middle Ages and even in the sixteenth and seventeenth centuries cats, especially black ones, were linked with witches and also the devil, who was supposed to be friends with them. People thought

the shining eyes of the cat in the dark were the fires of hell. If you owned a cat, you would be thought a witch! (But lots of harmless old ladies were called witches anyway!) Witches were supposed to be able to change themselves into animals, and their cats were often seen as the devil himself. Many people refused to talk when a cat was near, in case the "devil" heard their secrets!

Cats were also thought to be like ghosts, because they appear and disappear so soundlessly, just like ghosts.

A Norse legend has it that the goddess Freya had her chariot pulled by black cats. When the country converted to Christianity, Freya became a witch and her black cats were black horses who were very very swift and possessed by the devil. After seven years of service the horses were rewarded by being turned into witches, disguised as black cats.

In Mary Tudor's time cats were burned as they were seen as a symbol of Protestantism. When Elizabeth I came along, they burnt cats because they thought they were the symbol of the Roman Catholic faith! In France they had burnt so many cats by the year 1400, that when the Plague struck there were hardly any cats left to catch the rats that carried it!

Q. What's furry, has whiskers and chases outlaws?
A. *A posse cat.*

The Cat

Within that porch, across the way,
I see two naked eyes this night;
Two eyes that neither shut nor blink,
Searching my face with a green light.

But cats to me are strange, so strange –
I cannot sleep if one is near;
And though I'm sure I see those eyes,
I'm not so sure a body's there!

W. H. Davies

Here comes a shadow
Creeping black and slow.
I think it is my pussy cat,
But then, you never know.

Tabinka, The Witch's Cat

by Marie Stern

No one was as vain as Tabinka, who walked with her nose in the air and her tail in the air and never spoke to anyone. She was black, black, black, and her eyes were yellow, yellow, and one of her ears was orange. And I'll tell you why she was so vain. It was because she belonged to a witch, that was why!

Every night Tabinka went to sit by the fire near her mistress the witch, in her house of shale. Tabinka purred and purred but she never miaowed because – Tabinka had no voice! Every night she pleaded in cat signs, curling her tail around the witch's ankle, begging her to teach her magic or to give her back her voice so that she could tell everyone in the village who she was. But the witch would only say, "I will not teach you magic, you are only a cat, and I will keep your voice because it is better if no one knows whose cat you are. Come, have your nice little mousie tails, that's a good girl!"

That very moment, two little boys were looking in through the window and they heard it all and they ran back and told everybody all about it. The next time Tabinka went into the village, black, black, black, with her nose and tail in the air, the children laughed at her and cried, "Speak up, Tabinka!"

That night Tabinka would not purr, nor would she eat. Instead she hid in the coal scuttle and watched the witch do her magic. The witch took a ball of black wool from her pocket and she began to unwind it. As she did she rewound it into another ball chanting, "Black, black, whatever is black be silent." Then she threw the ball into the scuttle, not knowing Tabinka was there.

Next she swung a boiling pot of soup away from the fire, waved a broomstraw over it, and said, "Pot be cold!" The pot cooled right away. It was only a little witchcraft, just enough for the evening. She ate some soup and went to bed.

Tabinka crept out of the scuttle and waved a broomstraw over the same pot, which now stood cold on the table. "Pot be hot!" she purred. At once the pot boiled up and began to steam. Tabinka was beside herself with joy. She took the ball of wool out of the scuttle and unwound it and rewound it, purring, "Black, black, whatever is black be *White!*" And the wool understood, for it turned white and so did Tabinka! So she rewound the wool once more, pleading and purring, "White, white, whatever is white *Speak!*" Suddenly she felt a tickle in her throat and she said, "Mi-aooow-w!"

At the same time the white face on the clock said, "Ding, ding!" The white eggs in the cupboard broke open; the white goose in the back yard hissed and the white hair on the head of the witch cried, "Wake up, mistress! Your cat can speak!"

The witch jumped out of bed and Tabinka jumped out of the window. Then the witch smelled the hot soup in the pot. She could not resist tasting it and it burned her mouth so that she could not say her spells. Still, she was a witch. She pulled her left ear, and her mouth was healed. She seized the ball of wool which was on the table and began to wind and unwind it, saying, "Black, black, whatever is black . . ." but she forgot the wool was now *White*, so her spell was positively broken.

Tabinka became a very usual cat with a good miaowing voice. She remained white, and to the end of her days she still had one orange ear. Nobody minded because she was no longer proud; just very happy.

The Cat and the Devil

by James Joyce

Beaugency is a tiny old town on a bank of the Loire, France's longest river. It is also a very wide river, for France at least. At Beaugency it is so wide that if you wanted to cross it from one bank to the other you would have to take at least one thousand steps.

Long ago, the people of Beaugency, when they wanted to cross it, had to go in a boat for there was no bridge. And they could not make one for themselves or pay anyone else to make one. So what were they to do?

The devil, who is always reading the newspapers, heard about this sad state of theirs so he dressed himself and came to call on the local mayor of Beaugency, who was named Monsieur Alfred Byrne. This lord mayor was very fond of dressing himself too. He wore a scarlet robe and always had a great golden chain round his neck even when he was fast asleep in bed with his knees in his mouth.

The devil told the lord mayor what he had read in the newspaper and said he could make a bridge for the people of Beaugency so that they could cross the river as often as they wished. He said he could make as good a bridge as ever was made, and make it in one single night. The lord mayor asked him how much money he wanted for making such a bridge. "No money at all," said the devil, "all I ask is that the first person who crosses the bridge shall belong to me." "Good," said the lord mayor.

The night came down, all the people in Beaugency went to bed and slept. And when they put their heads out of their windows they cried: "O Loire, what a fine bridge!" For they saw a fine strong stone bridge thrown across the wide river.

All the people ran down to the head of the bridge and looked across it. There was the devil, standing on the other side of the bridge, waiting for the first person who should cross it. But nobody dared to cross it for fear of the devil.

Then there was a sound of bugles – that was a sign for the people to be silent – and the lord mayor M. Alfred Byrne appeared in his great scarlet robe and wearing his heavy gold chain round his neck. He had a bucket of water in one hand and under his arm – the other arm – he carried a cat.

The devil stopped dancing when he saw him from the other side of the bridge and put up his long spyglass.

All the people whispered to one another and the cat looked up at the lord mayor because in the town of Beaugency it was allowed that a cat should look at a lord mayor. When he was tired of looking at the lord mayor (because even a cat gets tired of looking at a lord mayor) he began to play with the lord mayor's heavy chain.

When the lord mayor came to the head of the bridge every man held his breath and every woman held her tongue.

The lord mayor put the cat down on the bridge and, quick as a thought, splash! he emptied the whole bucket of water over it.

The cat who was now between the devil and the bucket of water made up his mind quite as quickly and ran with his ears back across the bridge and into the devil's arms.

The devil was as angry as the devil himself. And off he went with the cat.

And since that time the people of that town are called *les chats* (cats) of Beaugency.

But the bridge is there still and there are boys walking and riding and playing upon it.

10

CATS FOR LUCK

How did cats, especially black ones, come to bring good luck, if they were linked with black magic and witches? This is because, if you saw a black cat in front of you, you had to say "black cat bring me luck" or stroke it three times and make a wish, or else the devil would bring you bad luck! If a black cat ran away, or crossed your path from left to right (not right to left) this was a bad omen, so you had to turn around three times!

There are lots of superstitions around the world about cats. Some are based on fact, most are not!

In the United States and Europe it is a white cat that is lucky, if it crosses your path, not a black cat, as in Britain and Japan. A black cat in America is bad luck!

A three-coloured cat will stop your house from catching fire.

In Russia, it is good luck to take a cat with you, if you want to be happy in a new house.

It is bad luck to carry a cat indoors, or to dream of one.

Kittens born in May bring bad luck. The Celts thought they brought snakes into the house!

It is not a good omen to hear a cat cry before you set off on a journey.

But it is a good omen if a cat sneezes near a bride on her wedding-day. And if a bachelor accidentally steps on a cat's tail, he will soon marry! In Wales, if you feed your cat well, it will be sunny on your wedding-day. The family cat at a wedding will bring good luck too.

A cat sneezing is a sign of rain. So also if it washes behind its ears three times; licks its tail; or sits with its back to the fire. This can also mean a frost is coming. A restless cat means a storm is brewing; so does a cat with its tail towards the fire. The Japanese think tortoiseshell cats drive storm devils away. If a cat cleans its face before it eats, better weather is on the way. If your cat claws at the curtain and carpets, then windy weather is coming! (Perhaps its claws need cutting?) In Eastern Europe, people used to throw their cats out of doors in thunderstorms, to quieten the god of lightning!

Kicking a cat brings on rheumatism. A good cure for a fever is to be washed in water that has been thrown at a cat! (How do you catch the water?) In Japan, cats are supposed to cure tummy ache and epilepsy. A single hair from a black cat's tail can cure a swollen eye-lid.

If your next-door neighbour's cat comes round, the neighbours are talking about you! It is good luck if a strange black cat visits you, but bad luck if it decides to stay!

In China, a cat washing its face means a stranger is coming.

In France, at one time, if they wanted a good harvest they decorated their cats with ribbons and flowers!

It is always good luck to take a cat on board with you if you are the captain of a ship. It is bad luck to say the word "cat" aloud on board, or to throw a cat overboard! If the cat starts jumping around, a storm is brewing. If it miaows, the voyage will not be easy. Sailors' wives used to keep black cats to bring good luck to their husbands, and to bring them home safely.

In Russia, it is good luck to put a cat into a baby's cradle, to drive away evil spirits. But some people think that black cats at Hallowe'en perch on sleeping babies and suck the breath out of them. Cats, it is true, do like warm places to sleep in, so it is best to put a cat-net over a cradle or pram, in case they accidentally sit on the baby!

Killing a cat brings bad luck; drown one and the devil will get you.

If a cat jumps over a dead body, the corpse will become a vampire. The only solution is to stop the funeral, catch and kill the cat, and start again. But killing a cat is bad luck!

Q. What did the flea say to his girl-friend?
A. *Shall we walk or take a cat?*

Q. What do cats say when they have their photos taken?
A. *"Mice!"*

Q. What does an old cat tell a young cat?
A. *"One swallow does not make a supper;" and "A mouse in the paws is worth two in the kitchen."*

Puss in Boots

by Charles Perrault

Once there was a miller who had three sons. When he died, he left the mill to his eldest son, a donkey to the second, but for the youngest son there was only a cat.

The poor lad was very disappointed. "What use is an old flea-bitten cat? Why, there isn't even enough fur on him to make me a hat!"

Hearing this, the cat said, "Master, don't despair. If you get me a pair of fine boots and a sack, I will make your fortune."

The miller's son had nothing to lose, so he did as the cat said. The cat put on his fine new boots, slung the sack over his shoulder and strode off to a rabbit warren nearby. In no time at all, Puss in Boots (as he was now called) caught two rabbits. He threw them in the sack and went to the king's palace and asked to speak to the king.

"Your Majesty," he said and gave a low bow. "I bring you these rabbits as a gift from my master, the Marquis of Carabas." The king was very pleased and told Puss to thank his master.

The next day Puss brought the king two pheasants, with the compliments of his master, and once again the king was pleased.

This continued until one day Puss overheard that the king and his daughter, the beautiful princess, were planning to drive along the river in their carriage. Puss ran to his master and said, "Our time has come. Go quickly and bathe in the river and leave the rest to me." The miller's son wondered at the cat but did as he was told.

As the king and princess were driving near the river, they heard a cry. "Help! Help! My master, the Marquis of Carabas is drowning!" It was Puss in Boots. He told the king that thieves had stolen his master's clothes while he was bathing. (In fact, Puss had hidden them himself.) The king ordered his men to rescue the marquis from the river and to fetch him some clothes from the palace.

When the miller's son was dressed in royal clothes, he looked very handsome indeed. The princess fell in love with him instantly and persuaded her father to invite him to ride with them. The king thanked the marquis graciously for all the gifts his cat had brought.

Meanwhile, Puss in Boots ran ahead until he came to some haymakers in a field. He said to them, "The king is coming. If he asks you who owns these fields, you must answer that it is the Marquis of Carabas. If you do not, I will scratch your eyes out!" Then Puss ran on until he came to some woodcutters in a forest and he said the same thing to them. And he continued until he reached some fishermen by a lake and he also told them to say the same thing.

Finally, Puss reached the castle of an ogre who owned all the surrounding lands. Although he was quaking in his boots, Puss hailed the ogre boldly.

Seen in *The Daily Mews*: "Wanted: a Cat for Light Mousework".

"Mummy, Mummy, there's a black cat in the kitchen!"
"That's all right dear, black cats are lucky."
"This one is – it's eaten the turkey!"

"Greetings, sir, I have heard you have the amazing power to change yourself into a tiger. Surely, this can't be true?"

"Indeed, it is," replied the ogre and instantly turned himself into a ferocious tiger.

"That is truly remarkable," said Puss. "But, surely, it is impossible for you to take the shape of a tiny mouse?"

The ogre snorted. "Why, nothing could be easier," and he changed into a tiny mouse. In a split second Puss pounced on the mouse and swallowed him in one gulp. And that was the end of the ogre.

In the meantime, the king's carriage had reached the hay fields.

"Who owns these fields full of hay?" asked the king.

"The Marquis of Carabas!" the haymakers replied.

"Who owns this forest full of straight timber?" asked the king.

"The Marquis of Carabas!" the woodcutters replied.

And the king's carriage drove on until it reached the lake.

"Who owns this lake full of fish?" asked the king.

"The Marquis of Carabas!" the fishermen replied.

The king turned to the marquis and said, "I must congratulate you on your great wealth."

By this time the king's carriage had arrived at the ogre's castle. Puss in Boots greeted them at the gate saying, "Your Majesty, welcome to the castle of my master, the Marquis of Carabas!" The king was amazed. The miller's son was even more amazed at his clever cat but he said nothing.

They entered the great hall and sat down to a magnificent feast. It was not long before the miller's son (now truly a marquis) asked to marry the princess and the king was only too glad to consent.

As for Puss in Boots, well, he was the guest of honour at their wedding and danced in his fine boots, of course. And he never chased mice again except for fun.

11
CATS
WITH NINE LIVES

Cats don't really have nine lives: it's just that nine is a very lucky number in many countries all over the world. And cats seem to be incredibly lucky in surviving all sorts of cat-astrophes!!

There are lots of true stories about cats who walk hundreds of miles back to their old homes or old owners. McCavity walked 500 miles from Scotland to Truro in three weeks; Sugar, born with a deformed hip, walked 1500 km from California to Oklahoma, to her owners' new home. How did she know where they were? How did Chat Beau, who walked from Louisiana to Texas, Smoky, who walked from Tulsa to Tennessee, and Pooh, who walked from Georgia to South Carolina? Rusty from Chicago must have hitched rides on trains and trucks to reach Boston, 950 miles away, in just eighty-three days. There is a nice story about an Alsatian and cat in a French village who were separated when their owners moved house. The dog disappeared one day, and turned up seven weeks later with the cat, having walked 140 miles to his old home to fetch her, and back again!

Tiger travelled on the roof-rack of his family's car for a hundred miles along the M6!

Peter, a ship's cat, survived a shipwreck in the River Rhine for eight days in an air pocket under water.

Hamlet travelled 60,000 miles round the world in the cargo hold of a British Airways plane.

Poor Patricia, thrown off a bridge in Oregon, USA, survived the fall of sixty-two metres. Gros Minou in Quebec, Canada, fell from a twentieth floor balcony, at a height of sixty-one metres, and lived to tell the tale. Tabby, in Sydney, fell down a drainpipe for fifteen metres, and got stuck, until rescued with a tin-opener! One cat fell down a quarry shaft in West Yorkshire and was rescued eighteen months later! One cat went up a tree, and stayed there for six years!

Curiosity has nearly killed many cats, but not quite! Timmy the cat was accidentally bricked up in a wall for twenty-four days; Victa was frozen in a fridge for twelve hours; Harvey, a Persian kitten, was washed in the automatic for ten minutes. One cat survived temperatures of 315°C (600°F) in an Ohio brick-kiln! Sedgewick received a 33,000 volt shock in a Cambridgeshire power station and survived. How shocking!

Q. When is it bad luck to see a cat?
A. *When you are a mouse.*

A cat in despondency sighed
And resolved to commit suicide
She passed under the wheels
Of eight automobiles
And after the ninth one she died.

Diddlety, diddlety, dumpty
The cat ran up the plum tree;
Half a crown
To fetch her down.
Diddlety, diddlety, dumpty.

There was a young person of Smyrna,
Whose grandmother threatened to burn her;
But she seized on the cat,
And said, "Granny, burn that!
You incongruous old woman of Smyrna!"

Edward Lear

Ding, dong, bell, pussy's in the well.
Who put her in? Little Johnny Green.
Who pulled her out? Little Tommy Stout.
What a naughty boy was that,
To try to drown poor pussy cat,
Who never did any harm,
But killed the mice in his father's barn.

The Cricket Match

He was a most conceited cat
Who thought he could play cricket.
With the first ball he was nearly out –
'Twas a case of paws before wicket.

When later he missed a lovely catch
In this the great cats' cricket match,
The rest of the kittens with good cause
Shouted out loudly, "Butter paws."

Q. What is worse than it raining cats and dogs?
A. *Hailing taxis.*

Three Tabbies

Three tabbies took out their cats to tea,
As well-behaved tabbies as well could be:
Each sat in the chair that each preferred,
They mewed for their milk, and they sipped and
purred.
Now tell me this (as these cats you've seen them) –
How many lives had these cats between them?

Kate Greenaway

The Cats of Kilkenny

There were once two cats of Kilkenny,
Each thought there was one cat too many;
So they fought and they fit,
And they scratched and they bit,
Till, excepting their nails
And the tips of their tails,
Instead of two cats, there weren't any.

A Mystery

Now, don't be in a hurry! Oh, I know what you
will say –
That I must be a very careless cat!
But I am not to blame for having dropped this
stupid tray,
And I will soon convince you as to that!

I simply carried it along, with careful steps and slow,
Till – ah! *I thought I smelt a smell of MOUSE!*
And then, just how it happened – well, I really do
not know –
There came a crash that seemed to shake the house.

And look at all the broken things, and all the
dreadful mess!
Oh, tell me what you think I'd better do!
What caused the tray to fall like that? I've tried for
hours to guess!
How *did* it drop? I cannot tell! Can you?

The King of the Cats

by Amabel Williams-Ellis

There was once, in a certain parish in England, a man whose job it was to ring the bell for the service, to look after the churchyard and dig the grave when anyone had to be buried.

He lived with his wife near the church, and they had a very fine cat – coal-black he was, with one white spot on his chest, and his name was Old Tom.

One winter's evening when the man had been out most of the day digging a grave, his wife and Old Tom sat by the fire waiting to have their tea till he should come back. They waited, and they waited, and still he didn't come, but at last, in he rushed, calling out:

"Who's Tom Tildrum?" and he looked so wild that both his wife and the cat fairly stared at him.

"What's the matter?" asked his wife.

"I've just heard and seen such queer things, you'd hardly believe!" said the man.

"Sit down quick, then, and tell us about it," said his wife.

Well, the man was in a great hurry to tell and though the kettle was boiling he sat down at once, opposite his wife, with Old Tom on the hearth-rug between them.

Q. What do you call someone who steals a pint of milk and a saucer?
A. *A cat-burglar.*

"I was busy digging a grave," says he, "for that old fellow that's to be buried tomorrow, and I'd gone down pretty well as deep as need be, it was getting dusk and I was standing down in the grave, shovelling out the last spadefuls, when I heard a something calling out 'Miaow'."

"Miaow," said Old Tom, as if in answer.

"Yes! Just like that," said the man nodding. "So I looked up and what do you think I saw?"

"How can I tell?" answered his wife.

"Well, it was nine black cats, each one with a white spot on his chest, just like our Old Tom, and what do you think they were doing? They were carrying a little small coffin. It was covered with a black velvet pall and on the lid was a little small crown. They were coming along very slowly, and at every third step they all called out, 'Miaow!' "

"Miaow!" said Old Tom again.

"Yes! Just like that," said the man. "Well, they were coming nearer and it seemed as if they were going to pass quite close, and I could see that eight of them were carrying the coffin, and that the ninth – the biggest one – was walking in front for all the world like . . . But wife! Just look at our Old Tom! You'd think he was listening to every word!"

"Never mind Old Tom," said his wife. "Go on."

"Well, there they were, coming nearer and nearer, and at every third step crying, 'Miaow' . . ."

"Miaow!" cried out Old Tom again.

"Yes, just like that," said the man, "and just as they were going past the grave where I stood watching them, they all stopped and they all looked straight at me . . . But wife! Just look at Old Tom! He's looking at me just as they did!"

"Go on, for pity's sake!" cried his wife. "Never mind Old Tom."

"Well then, the one that was walking in front – the one that *wasn't* carrying the coffin it was – came up close, and it said to me – yes, I tell you, it *said* to me, in a squeaky voice, 'Tell Tom Tildrum that Tim Toldrum's dead!' But, oh dear wife! How can I tell Tom Tildrum that Tim Toldrum's dead, if I don't know who Tom Tildrum is?"

"Look at Old Tom!" called out his wife. "Just look at Old Tom!"

And well they might look! For Old Tom was standing up, and his fur was stiff on his back, and he was looking twice the size, and his tail was like a big black bottle-brush, and his great green eyes were staring at them. And then, as they watched him, what did he do but call out in a squeaky voice:

"If Tim Toldrum is dead, then I'm the King of the Cats!"

And with that, up the chimney he sprang and they never saw him again.

12
STAR CATS

It has always been very lucky for a theatre to have its own cat backstage. Of course, the theatre cat was useful for keeping mice away! It is bad luck, though, for a cat to go on the stage itself. In London's theatreland there is Beerbohm at the Globe Theatre; Fleur at the Lyric; Tabitha at the Phoenix; Bouncer at the Fortune; Plug at the Adelphi; Smoky at the Strand; Ambrose at Drury Lane; Cleo and Chico at the Dominion and Polly and Victoria at the Apollo. As Hamlet would say: Tabby or not tabby?

The photo of Beerbohm, named after a famous actor-manager, hangs in the foyer, and he often comes on stage! He sometimes joins in the performance, especially when there is singing! Perhaps he would like the Cat Duet by Rossini, which is just a lot of miaows! Beerbohm once used the stage set as a litter tray, though!

Bouncer at the Fortune is now retired, but he used to help with the publicity for the musical *Cats* by Andrew Lloyd Webber. This exceedingly popular rock-musical has been running in London for over ten years now! It is also showing all round the world.

Q. What kind of cat enjoys bowling?
A. *An alley cat.*

Cats is actually based on a collection of poems for children by the famous poet T. S. Eliot, called *Old Possum's Book of Practical Cats* (1939). One of Eliot's poems actually has a theatre cat as the hero: Gus, whose name is really Asparagus, and who was "once a Star of the highest degree":

In the Pantomime season I never fell flat,
And I once understudied Dick Whittington's Cat.
But my grandest creation, as history will tell,
Was Firefrorefiddle, the Fiend of the Fell.

Dick Whittington is certainly a very popular panto-mime at Christmas. There was a real Dick Whittington, born in the fourteenth century, who did become Lord Mayor of London – three times. There is a picture of him in Westminster Abbey. His famous cat (Miss Puss) was probably not real, but the story goes that he bought her for a penny when he came to London. There is a statue of her on the top of Highgate Hill, where Dick "turned again" after listening to the bells.

There are famous actor cats in films and on television. The most famous advertising cat was Arthur, the Spillers cat food cat with a lovely white coat. He appeared in adverts eighteen weeks a year, scooping food out of a Kattomeat tin with his paw. He was also in thirty-five films! He was once kidnapped (catnapped?) and had his life-story written. He died in 1976, aged nearly seventeen. Arthur II appeared in 1987.

Another busy performer was a white Persian called Solomon, who appeared in the James Bond films *Diamonds are Forever* and *You Only Live Twice*; and

Stanley Kubrick's *A Clockwork Orange*. He was very well known in Britain for advertising Kosset carpets.

Did you know that there is an Oscar for animals? It is called a "Patsy" (Picture Animal Top Star of the Year)! One cat won a Patsy for its performance in *Breakfast at Tiffany's* (1962); and one for playing an alley cat called Rhubarb in 1951.

The most famous film cats have been cartoon cats. The first cartoon cats appeeared soon after the beginning of this century. The British cat-artist Louis Wain made *Pussyfoot* at Shepperton in 1916; in America there was a black moggie Krazy Kat in 1916. More popular, with a huge fan club, was Felix the Cat in the 1920s. There is a brand of cat food still named after him. In the 1960s he went on television. Everyone still laughs at the antics of Tom and Jerry, the famous cat and mouse, first created in the late 1930s by the film cartoonists William Hanna and Joseph Barbera for MGM, and who performed in over 150 films! The Hanna-Barbera team also came up with the very successful TV cat called Top Cat (or TC to his friends), a cool, street-wise alley cat. And we musn't forget Sylvester, with a lisp, and Tweetie Pie the canary ("I tought I taw a puddy tat") who first came on the screen for Warner Brothers in 1944. Walt Disney gave us *The Aristocats* (1970), a full-length film, with Thomas O'Malley, another alley cat, and the Duchess.

In comic-strips there has been Korky the Cat, and King Kat. But the most famous strip-cartoon cat in the world today is the lazy orange monster Garfield, who first appeared in the United States in 1978. Four years later, his face was in a thousand newspapers all over the world, and now his grinning face and catty comments are all over our pencil boxes, satchels, mugs and T-shirts!

Q. What is a cat's favourite TV programme?
A. *The Mews at Ten.*

Q. What else?
A. *Miami Mice.*

The Cheshire Cat

by Lewis Carroll

Alice was a little startled by seeing the Cheshire Cat sitting on a bough of a tree a few yards off . . .

The cat only grinned when it saw Alice. It looked good-natured, she thought: still it had *very* long claws and a great many teeth, so she felt that it ought to be treated with respect.

"Cheshire Puss," she began, rather timidly, as she did not at all know whether it would like the name: however, it only grinned a little wider. "Come, it's pleased so far," thought Alice, and she went on. "Would you tell me, please, which way I ought to go from here?"

"That depends a good deal on where you want to get to," said the Cat.

"I don't much care where—" said Alice.

"Then it doesn't matter which way you go," said the Cat.

"—so long as I get *somewhere*," Alice added as an explanation.

"Oh, you're sure to do that," said the Cat, "if you only walk long enough."

Alice felt that this could not be denied, so she tried another question. "What sort of people live about here?"

"In *that* direction," the Cat said, waving its right paw round, "lives a Hatter: and in *that* direction," waving the other paw, "lives a March Hare. Visit either you like; they're both mad."

"But I don't want to go among mad people," Alice remarked.

"Oh, you can't help that," said the Cat. "We're all mad here. I'm mad. You're mad."

"How do you know I'm mad?" said Alice.

"You must be," said the Cat, "or you wouldn't have come here."

Q. What is a cat's favourite pantomime?
A. *Dick Whittington and his Cat.*

Alice didn't think that proved it at all: however, she went on: "And how do you know that you're mad?"

"To begin with," said the Cat, "a dog's not mad. You grant that?"

"I suppose so," said Alice.

"Well, then," the Cat went on, "you see a dog growls when it's angry and wags its tail when it's pleased. Now I growl when I'm pleased, and wag my tail when I'm angry. Therefore I'm mad."

"I call it purring, not growling," said Alice.

"Call it what you like," said the Cat. "Do you play croquet with the Queen today?"

"I should like it very much," said Alice, "but I haven't been invited yet."

"You'll see me there," said the Cat, and vanished.

Alice was not much surprised at this, she was getting so well used to queer things happening. While she was still looking at the place where it had been, it suddenly appeared again.

"By-the-bye, what became of the baby?" said the Cat. "I'd nearly forgotten to ask."

"It turned into a pig," Alice answered very quietly, just as if the Cat had come back in a natural way.

"I thought it would," said the Cat, and vanished again.

Alice waited a little, half expecting to see it again, but it did not appear, and after a minute or two she walked on in the direction in which the March Hare was said to live. "I've seen hatters before," she said to herself: "The March Hare will be much the most interesting, and perhaps, as this is May, it won't be raving mad – at least not so mad as it was in March." As she said this, she looked up, and there was the Cat again, sitting on a branch of a tree.

"Did you say 'pig' or 'fig'?" said the Cat.

"I said 'pig'," replied Alice; "and I wish you wouldn't keep appearing and vanishing so suddenly: you make one quite giddy!"

"All right," said the Cat; and this time it vanished quite slowly, beginning with the end of the tail, and ending with the grin, which remained some time after the rest of it had gone.

"Well! I've often seen a cat without a grin," thought Alice; "but a grin without a cat! It's the most curious thing I ever saw in all my life!"

"Grinning like a Cheshire Cat"

This was a popular saying long before Lewis Carroll's *Alice in Wonderland*, which was written in the nineteenth century. That is probably why Lewis Carroll decided to put a Cheshire Cat into Alice's adventures. But nobody really knows where the phrase comes from. One suggestion is that it comes from "to grin like a Cheshire Caterling" – the name of a swordsman in the time of King Richard III, a protector of the royal forests, and famed for his evil grin. Another is that it refers to the open-mouthed animal on the coat of arms of the eleventh-century Earl of Chester in Cheshire.

There was also a special kind of Cheshire cheese which had a cat's face on it – but perhaps it was there because of the saying? I think the cheese holds a clue. My favourite suggestion is that cats in Cheshire grin because they have licked the cream that goes into the cheese for which Cheshire is famous.

Curtis The Hip-Hop Cat

Now this is the story of a Hip-Hop cat,
His name is Curtis and, boy, is he fat.
You'd think his hobby was putting on weight –
All that mattered to that cat was the food on his
plate.

His mum and dad shook their heads in despair:
"Why's our son such a slob? It really ain't fair."
Life wasn't much fun for this fat little cat
Till he saw a sight that just knocked him flat.

As Curtis was walking to the end of his street,
He saw these two cats dancing to the beat.
They balanced on their heads and spun like a top.
"Everyone knows we're the Sultans of Hip-Hop."

When Curtis showed all his friends at school
The other kits thought, "Breakdancing's cool!"
Now this new dance craze has hit the street
Everybody's looking for the Purrfect Beat.

Now this is the story of a Hip-Hop cat.
Get down, Curtis, and burn up the mat!

Curtis and his friends formed a breaking crew.
They went uptown to see how they could do.
They were popping and gyrating when who should
wander by
But the Sultans of Hip-Hop; and Curtis caught
their eye.

Now this is the story of a Hip-Hop cat.
Get down, Curtis, and burn up the mat!

"Hey, kits, you're lookin' fresh – we think your style
is great.
There's gonna be a jam, we'll let you know the
date."
Curtis told his crew, "We better had prepare
The Battle will be tough, all the baddest will be
there."

Now this is the story of a Hip-Hop cat.
Get down Curtis, and burn up the mat!

Q. What do you call a bald Cheshire Cat?
A. *Yul Grinner.*

What a frantic night! The shakedown of the year!
Cats came from all around and EVERYONE was
there.
Fresh Cream was there with her all-girl crew,
Grandmaster Scratch and the Sultans, too.

Now this is the story of a Hip-Hop cat.
You gotta rock it – pop it – and knock 'em flat!

The DJs mixed and the MCs rapped.
The battle started and everybody clapped.
The B-cats boogied and the beat went boom
Then all eyes turned to the centre of the room.

Now this is the story of a Hip-Hop cat.
You gotta rock it – pop it – and knock 'em flat!

Everyone could see throughout the whole contest,
Of all the crews, two were the best.
One was a posse that everybody knew.
The other crew was – check it out – guess who?

Now this is the story of a Hip-Hop cat.
You gotta rock it – pop it – and knock 'em flat!

It couldn't be decided, neither crew could fail,
Till Curtis showed his secret move – he spun upon
his TAIL!
The crowd went wild – he'd really shown them how.
There's no doubt that Curtis is the Hippest-Hop
cat now.

Now this is the story of a Hip-Hop cat.
You gotta rock it – pop it – and knock 'em flat!

So come on, you Hip-Hops – the moral of my tale
Is you can make it to the top, you don't have to fail.
When the world seems a mess, put on your
dancing shoes.
Boogie down everybody and chase away those blues.

Now that was the story of a Hip-Hop cat.
He's one of a kind – he's where it's at!

Gini Wade

13
CATTY FABLES FROM AESOP

Retold by Katie Wales

1. *The Cat and the Cock*

One day a cat made up his mind that he would eat a cockerel, so he took him by surprise one morning. When he had caught him, he asked the cock if he knew of any reason why he shouldn't be killed. The cock said that he made himself very useful to people by crowing in the early morning, and waking them up in time for work.

"That is exactly what I complain about!" said the cat. "You make such a terrible noise that nobody can sleep. Your own words show that you don't deserve to live." So he ate him all up.

Moral: A person who wants to do wrong can easily find an excuse for doing it.

2. *The Cat and the Mice*

A house was once so over-run with mice that the owner decided to get a cat, who killed and ate some of them each day. But the mice soon saw what was happening, and held a meeting to discuss what they should do. They agreed that no mouse was to go down further than the top shelf. This worked very well for the mice, but the cat grew hungry, because he had no mice to eat. So he made up a plan of his own. He hung down by his hind legs from a peg in the wall, pretending to be dead. He hoped that the mice would come down to the ground again. But he was disappointed. One wise old mouse peeped over the edge of the shelf and said: "There you are, are you! Well, you can stay there. We wouldn't come near you, even if you were stuffed with straw!"

Moral: We learn by experience.

3. *The Cat and the Fox*

A cat and a fox one day were discussing together who would come off better, if they found themselves in trouble. "Well," said the fox, "I have a whole bag of tricks I could use." Just then a pack of hounds came running towards them at full cry. The cat immediately ran up a tree; but the fox was too slow, and was torn to pieces on the spot. Said the cat to himself: "One sure trick is better than a hundred slippery ones."

Moral: Nature has provided for us better than we could have done for ourselves.

14

TAIL-PIECES

A cat makes about a dozen different tail movements!

An upright tail is a sign of greeting; a waving tail a sign of anger. But when a cat waves just the tip of its tail, then this is a sign of pleasure or friendship. A quivering tail means excitement. The cat will also wag its tail slowly from side to side when it is crouched in the grass, stalking a mouse or bird or butterfly.

A cat with its eyes closed may not be asleep. Watch its tail – if it moves, the cat is really awake, on the alert.

When a tom cat holds his tail forward over his head, he is the "top cat" in his patch.

An upright tail with the back arched right up and ears back means the cat is ready for attack! When the fur on its tail and back literally "stands on end", then it is probably scared!

The Manx cat, of course, has no tail usually, so it is called a "rumpie". Some kinds of Manx cats have a tiny tail – so they are called "stumpies"! One story explains how Manx cats came to have no tails. In the olden days, the Manx warriors were very envious of the plumed helmets of their Irish and Danish enemies, so they used to kill cats for their tails. But in the end one wise mother cat had her litter of kittens on the top of Snaefell, and bit off their tails, so that the warriors would lose interest in them. From that day onwards, mother cats passed on the secret to their daughters, until eventually Manx kittens were actually born without tails.

In Japan there is the Bobtail cat, with a pom-pom tail. You will see it in Japanese paintings.

Q. Why is a cat like a gossipy person?
A. *Because it is a tail (tale)-bearer.*

There was a young tom cat named Tag
Who went to a shop for a flag
When the owner asked why,
He said with a sigh,
"I'm a Manx, so I've no tail to wag."

Someone Stole The

While I was taking a short   -nap
  someone stole the   ,
I should have spun round like a   herine wheel
when someone stole the   .
But I was too slow to   ch them,
  when someone stole the   .

Now the   amaran can't float,
  because someone stole the   .
And the   erpillar can't crawl,
  because someone stole the   .
And the   aract can't fall,
  because someone stole the   .

It was not me and it was not you
  but it is   egorically true,
And if you were to ask me
  I'd say it was a   astrophe
That someone's stolen the   .

                          Brian Patten

Q. Who was the most famous cat tyrant in
   history?
A. *Cattila the Hun.*

Did you hear about the cat who entered a milk-
drinking contest? He won by four laps.

Q. When a cat is on the fence, how is it like a ten-pence piece?
A. *Because its head is on one side, and its tail is on the other.*

Q. What do you get if you cross five legs, two tails, and a dozen whiskers?
A. *A cat with spare parts.*

Q. What did the cat say when it chased its tail?
A. *"This is the end."*

The author and the publishers wish to thank the following for permission to reproduce copyright material:

'I Have a Whiskery Kitten', Leila Berg. Reprinted with permission from Reed International Books Ltd from *Time For One More* (Magnet 1986). © 1948/51/57/59/80 and 86 Leila Berg.

'Pussy Cat Pussy Cat', Max Fatchen. Reprinted with permission from Penguin Books Ltd from *Wry Rhymes For Troublesome Times* (Viking Kestral 1983). © Max Fatchen 1983.

'This is My Chair', Paul Gallico. Reprinted in the UK with permission from Souvenir Press and in Canada with permission from Crown Publishers Inc from *Honourable Cat* (Heinemann 1972). © Paul Gallico 1972.

'Cat Poem', Adrian Henri. Reprinted with permission from Rogers, Coleridge and White Ltd from *The Mersey Sound* Revised Edition (Penguin 1983). © Adrian Henri 1983.

'Conversation on a Garden Wall', Adrian Henri. Reprinted with permission from Rogers, Coleridge and White Ltd from *The Phantom Lollypop Lady* (Methuen 1986). © Adrian Henri 1986.

'How the Cat Became', Ted Hughes. Reprinted with permission from Faber and Faber Ltd from *How The Whale Became And Other Stories* (Faber and Faber 1963). © Ted Hughes 1963.

Shark Infested Custard £2.50
Katie Wales

What's yellow and dangerous?
Yes . . . it's Shark Infested Custard -
the juiciest joke book ever!

Packed with a mouth-watering menu of delicious
food jokes to tickle your tastebuds.

It's a Joke Book to really get your teeth into!

The Joke Machine   £2.50

Chosen by children in aid of the Earl of Stockton Children's Fund and the Save the Children Fund

Q. What sits under the sea and shivers?
A. *A nervous wreck!*

Q. Why is a leg funny?
A. *Because it's got a bottom at the top!*

Q. What do you get when you sit under a cow?
A. *A pat on the head!*

And there's more where they came from in
The Joke Machine, illustrated by Tony Ross.

Madabout Monsters £2.99
Mary Danby

What are YOU mad about?
Are you dotty about Dracula? Or wild about
werewolves? Are you eager for ogres? A
Frankenstein fan? Do you know the difference
between a sasquatch and a squonk?

If you'd like to meet a whole crowd of peculiar
creatures, and if you're looking for jokes, poems,
stories, Abominable Snowmen or Zombies . . .

YOU MUST BE MAD ABOUT MONSTERS!

Madabout Ghosts   £2.99
Mary Danby

What are YOU mad about?
Do you believe in spooks and spectres and headless
horsemen? Could you spend a night in a haunted
house?

If the eerie world of the supernatural makes your
blood run cold and you LIKE being scared by
creepy stories, poems, jokes and puzzles . . .

YOU MUST BE MAD ABOUT GHOSTS!

CARToon

Heroes